Math
Made Simple

Grade 1

Written by
Kaye Furlong and Margaret Hupp
Illustrated by Fran Newman D'Amico

D0875038

FS-23201 Math Made Simple Grade 1
All rights reserved–Printed in the U.S.A.
Copyright © 1997 Frank Schaffer Publications, Inc.
23740 Hawthorne Blvd.
Torrance, CA 90505

Introduction

Math plays a vital role in everyone's life on a daily basis—in a variety of situations. It is, therefore, absolutely a necessity that children develop, understand, and learn to apply math skills.

What time is it?

How many months are in a year?

How many dimes are in one dollar?

These and other questions are children's attempts to make sense of mathematical concepts.

Math Made Simple has been designed to help students develop a basic understanding of math concepts and to help them practice skills and algorithms related to those concepts. The activities presented in this book help students learn to apply these skills and concepts in a variety of problem solving situations.

The objective of *Math Made Simple* is to help all students succeed in math. In order to ensure success for all learners, the activities in this book are presented in a variety of formats.

The book is divided into five sections. In the front of each section are Teacher Resource pages. These pages feature many exciting extension activities that you can guide the students to do. Another fascinating aspect of the Teacher Resource pages is the School-Home Connection activities. These activities provide a great way for students to apply the skills and concepts presented to situations at home. These kinds of activities are a great way to show students and their families that opportunities for learning math can arise at home as well as at school and that learning math can be interesting, fun, and valuable.

Behind the Teacher Resource pages are lots of fun and stimulating activity pages students can complete to learn the important math skills and concepts featured in the section. The activities include matching, coloring, playing games, completing dot-to-dots, drawing, creating shapes, measuring, and much more. These activities provide yet another exciting means for students to better understand the concepts and skills presented in each section.

The concepts covered in *Math Made Simple* are basic to most first grade mathematics programs. Students will develop conceptual understanding of and will practice skills relating to the following mathematical concepts: numeration, addition and subtraction, geometry, money, time, measurement, fractions, and calendars.

To reinforce the math topics presented in this book and to help students gain a greater understanding of these topics, prepare (or have the students prepare) math journals. These provide students with places to write down the thinking processes or steps that they have used to solve problems. They are also wonderful places for students to record any interesting mathematical discoveries they make. Let the students share their journals with each other and with you when applicable.

Another valuable tool you and the students can make are erasable cards (i.e., laminated pieces of paper). These are great for students to use when doing group activities. Students can write down answers to problems using crayons and hold them up. This enables you to quickly check to see who understands the concept being presented. Smaller groups can then be created to reteach a particular skill.

Regardless of your reasons for implementing *Math Made Simple*, you will be delighted as you watch your students discover how interesting and fun learning math can be!

Numeration

The activities in this section are perfect to help students understand the number system, especially place value and relationship of numbers. This understanding will provide students with a foundation they can use to develop skills in computation. A solid knowledge of place value also provides a good foundation to help students order and compare numbers. Daily experiences help children see the connection between math and real life.

CONCEPTS

The ideas and activities presented in this section will help students explore the following concepts:
- number lines
- counting to 100
- ordering numbers
- counting by twos, fives, and tens
- greater than, less than
- tallying
- odd and even numbers
- ordinals to tenth

GROUP LEARNING
Class Activities

Through the Year Number Line
Secure a roll of adding machine tape (or something similar) to the bulletin board above the calendar by tying string through it so that it is easy to pull. Each day, pull out approximately 2–3 inches of tape. Write the number of the day of school on the tape using a black marker. As the days of school increase, you will have a meaningful number line. It will be a great reference for the students. If you have room, put a small picture over days on which special events occurred. At the end of the year, review this with the students.

Counting Backwards
As soon as you have a few numbers on your number line, have the students count aloud forwards and backwards. Point to the numbers as the students count.

Counting by 1's and 10's
Using a time line, circle day 10 with a bright color. Continue circling every 10th day (20th, 30th, etc.). Students can recite the numbers as you point to them. You can have a special action, such as a clap, each time you reach 10. Students can choose different actions for 10 if you wish to change to keep everyone interested. This idea works well using clocks and calendars, too.

"I SAW . . ."
Class Activity

Show a picture card that has a variety of objects on it to the class for one minute. Tell the students to try to remember all of the objects on the card. Remove the card. Have the students play "I saw . . ." aloud, or they can draw the objects they remember.

READING AND SHOWING CONCRETE NUMBERS

Manipulative Activity

Buy or make cards with numbers, number words, and pictures that indicate a number of things. Have the students show the number of things you ask for orally and using the cards. For example, if you say to the students, "Show 4," and show them the #4 card, they should take out 4 like objects (perhaps from collections of items they have) and set them on their desks.

Variation: Give the students more difficult directions as, "Show two more than one," or "Show one less than five," etc. The students determine the answer and show the number of items on their desks.

TALLY TIME

Directed Activity

Teach students to tally. To do this, have students, one at a time, stand up and come to the front of the room. Each time a student stands up, put a tally mark on the board. When you get to 5, explain that this is a group. Start a new group for 6–10. When you reach 10, circle the two fives. Keep tallying until you have used all the students in the class. Each time a new 10 is reached, circle it. Students will soon be able to recognize tens without counting.

COUNTING PRACTICE

Manipulative Activity

Students should have many opportunities to count aloud together. Give them time to count out objects from different collections of things (i.e., buttons) on their desks. For example, tell them to count out 30 things. Then have them put the objects in groups of 10 and count by tens. Next, have them put the objects in groups of 5 and count by fives, then twos, etc.

BOUNCE AND COUNT

Group Activity

In small groups, have students bounce a ball to each other. The bouncer says the first number, the receiver says the next, and so on up to 50, 100, etc. For more fun, have the students count by twos, fives, and tens whenever they are ready.

Class Activity

Toothpick Storybook

Provide each student with a 10-page book and cover using 6" x 9" sheets of construction paper. Each student can use toothpicks to show the numbers from 1–10. For example, on the first page, one toothpick is used, two are used on the second page, etc. Then tell the students to draw pictures incorporating the toothpicks into the pictures. The students can write or dictate one sentence about each picture such as "One makes a tree trunk." Each day, have the students add one page until they reach 10. Then let the students share their books with each other.

LEARNING TO WRITE NUMBERS

As soon as the students have an understanding of the meaning of numbers, teach them the *Number Song* below. As they learn the song, have them follow the directions in the song for writing the numbers. (Make sure you show students how to make the numbers as you go through the song the first time.) Students will be "sky writing" the numbers in the air. When you feel that they have the correct shapes, provide them with copies of page 6 that they can use to practice writing numbers and number words.

Number Song

(tune: "Skip to My Lou")

*Tell the students to follow the actions
in the song and move their arms in the air.*

A straight line down and that is all (sing 3 times)
To make the number one.

Halfway down and slide to the right (3 times)
To make the number two.

Around and in, around and up (3)
To make the number three.

Down and over, cut it in half (3)
To make the number four.

Down and around, put on a hat (3)
To make the number five.

Bring her down and give her a twirl (3)
To make the number six.

Over and down and that is all (3)
To make the number seven.

Make an S and slide back up (3)
To make the number eight.

Around and down and that is all (3)
To make the number nine.

I HAVE . . .

Class Activity

Make a set of cards that contains numbers having increments of five on them (5, 10, 15, etc.). Pass out the cards to the students. Pose such problems to the students as "I have 5 more than 50. What do I have?" The student with 55 then stands and says, "I have 55." Continue asking questions, until everyone has had a turn to stand. As soon as possible, have the students begin to ask their own questions. This game also works well using twos and tens.

Class Activity

Hands Around the Room

Have students trace around their hands and cut them out. Put the hands up around your room, counting by fives as you add a new hand (four fingers and a thumb). Ask questions such as, "How many would we have if someone new joined our class (+10), or if someone moved away (-10)." Students are now adding and subtracting larger numbers in their heads.

ODD AND EVEN NUMBERS

Learning Activities

- There are a lot of fun ways to teach the concept of odd and even numbers. One way is in conjunction with daily calendar activities. After learning about odd and even numbers, students can determine which days of the month and of the school year are odd and which are even.

- Another way is to have students line up in pairs. Explain that if one person doesn't have a partner, there is an odd number of students in the class. An even number of students means that all students will have partners. If you have an even number of students, add yourself as the odd person to demonstrate the concept of "odd" to the students.

- Yet another way to teach even and odd numbers is to have the students take a handful of objects and divide them into groups of two to discover if they have an odd or an even amount. Then have them count the objects. On the board or a chart, make a list of the even numbers and the odd numbers. Help the students discover how odd numbers end (1, 3, 5, 7, 9) and how even numbers end (0, 2, 4, 6, 8).

Whenever appropriate situations come up, ask the students if certain numbers are even or odd.

Group Activity

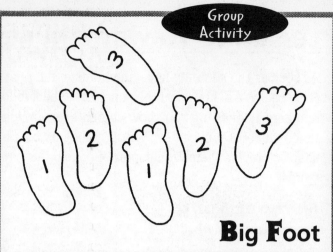

Big Foot

Cut feet patterns out of construction paper. Number them and give one to each student. Have the students line up in various ways, placing their feet in the correct order. For example, they can line up by ones, twos (even numbers only), fives, tens, etc. They can have a line of only odd numbers in order, next to a line of even numbers only. Have the students suggest ways to line up. Or, try having the student with number 10 come to the front. Then ask for the student with the next largest number to come up. This student stands to the right of the first student. Ask for the student with one less to come up and stand on the left. You could even have, for example, 17 and 19 stand with a space between them. Ask who can fill the space.

Matching Game

MATCH UP

Using a set of cards containing number words, matching numbers, and matching pictures, individual or pairs of students can practice matching the number words with the pictures and numerals. Color-code the cards on the back so the game is self-checking. This activity can also be used for such activities as matching facts.

Game

CREATIVE HOPSCOTCH

Using chalk, number a hopscotch game by twos, fives, or tens so students can practice skip counting as they jump. For more fun, make hopscotch games in different shapes with higher counting numbers.

FS-23201 Math Made Simple ■ © Frank Schaffer Publications, Inc.

HUNDREDS CHARTS ACTIVITIES

Class Activities

Give each student one copy of a hundreds chart and have him or her try the activities below.

Show Me—Before and After

Say a number out loud. Have the students put a marker on the number before and the number after. Call out larger and larger numbers as the year progresses. For example, "Show 27. Show one more. Show 72. Show one less. Show 65. Show two more." Make the questions include as much thinking as possible. Keep stretching the questions depending on the level of your class. Small groups can work with you or another adult if they are more advanced. Let students practice making up questions of their own to ask their group members.

What Number Am I?

Students can show answers for "What number am I?" questions such as, "I'm two more than 20. What number am I?", "I'm an even number that is more than 30, but less than 34. What number am I?"

Center Activity

CENTER FUN

Set up a center with 10 small cups, a variety of small objects (beans, buttons) to count, and copies of hundreds charts. Students can work with partners to count out 10 items into each cup. When the cups are filled with "tens," the students count by tens to 100. Students then color in the tens on the hundreds charts.

DANDY DEFINITIONS

Writing Activity

In their journals, have students write definitions for *odd* and *even numbers*. Tell students to give at least two examples of each number.

Homework

School-Home Connection

In a weekly or monthly letter to parents, encourage the parents to reinforce and extend the lessons you are teaching their children. Give parents specific ideas for questions they can ask their children or games they can play at home or while in the car. For example, when at the grocery store, parents can show their children prices of items such as those for two cereals. They can ask their children which costs more, which box contains more ounces, etc. Students can also practice writing missing numbers while the parents cook dinner. Parents can count to a given number, stop, and have their children say or write what comes next. The more specific examples you provide, the more likely parents will be to try some of these at home. Title the suggestions, "Help Your Child Get Ahead" or something similar that will let the parents know that they are helping their children be more successful.

Name_____

Matching Mania

Write the numbers and words. Match.

1 ___ ___

2 ___ ___ ___

3 ___ ___ ___

4 ___ ___ ___

5 ___ ___ ___

6 ___ ___ ___

7 ___ ___ ___

8 ___ ___ ___

9 ___ ___ ___

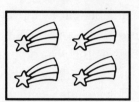

five

one

seven

two

nine

three

eight

four

six

FS-23201 Math Made Simple • © Frank Schaffer Publications, Inc.

What's Next?

A. Write the number
that comes after.

B. Write the number
that comes before.

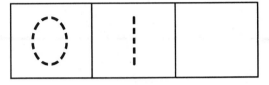

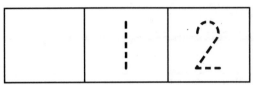

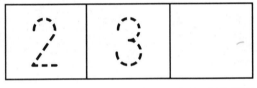

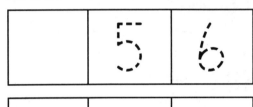

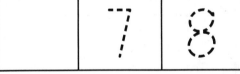

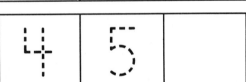

C. Count and write the numbers from 10–0 backwards.

Caught in the Middle

A. Write the number that comes . . .

before,			**between,**			**after.**		
5	6	7	6	7	8	7	8	9
8	9	10	5	6	7	1	2	3
0	1	2	8	9	10	4	5	6

B. Write the numbers from 10–0 backwards.

10, 9, 8, 7, 6, 5, 4, 3, 2, 1, 0

10, 9, 8, 7, 6, 5, 4, 3, 2, 1, 0

C. Draw.

three	nine ♡	seven ☺
five 🍎	eight	four ☁

Name_____

Partners

Draw lines to match partners.

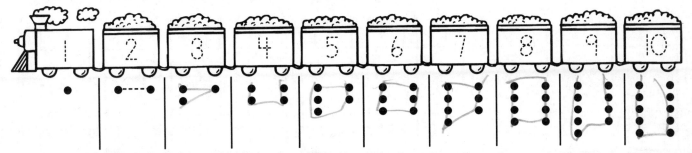

1. Color the even numbers yellow.

2. Color the odd numbers orange.

3. Write the even numbers.

____, ____, ____, ____, and ____

4. Write the odd numbers.

____, ____, ____, ____, and ____

5. Count the flowers. Circle **odd** or **even**.

odd
even

odd
even

odd
even

odd
even

odd
even

odd
even

odd
even

odd
even

odd
even

odd
even

Name_____

The Line Up

A. **before**   **after**   B. **before**   **after**

_____ 13 _____   _____ 11 _____

_____ 15 _____   _____ 14 _____

_____ 17 _____   _____ 19 _____

_____ 12 _____   _____ 16 _____

_____ 18 _____   _____ 10 _____

C. Count from 20–0 backwards.

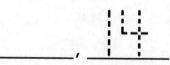

20 , _____ , 18 , _____ , _____ , _____ , 14 ,

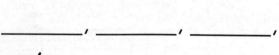
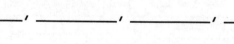

_____ , _____ , _____ , _____ , 9 , _____ ,

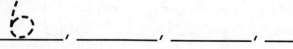
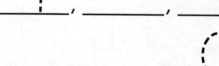

6 , _____ , _____ , _____ , _____ , _____ , 0

FS-23201 Math Made Simple ▪ © Frank Schaffer Publications, Inc.

What's Missing?

1. Write the missing numbers.

21				25				30

2. Write the numbers before and after.

___ 26 ___   ___ 22 ___   ___ 29 ___

3. Write the missing numbers.

31					37			

4. Write the numbers before and after.

___ 36 ___   ___ 32 ___

___ 37 ___   ___ 39 ___

Count Down!

1. Write the missing numbers.

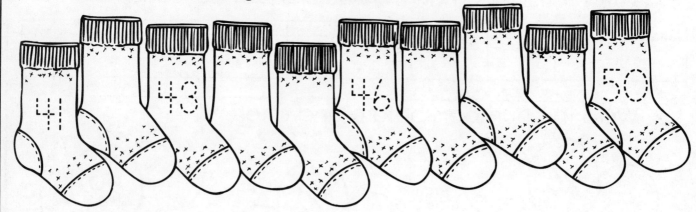

41   43   46   50

2. Write the numbers by twos to 50.

___2___, ___4___, _____, _____, _____, ___12___, _____, _____, _____,

_____, ___22___, _____, _____, _____, ___32___, _____,

_____, ___40___, _____, _____, _____, ___50___

3. Write the missing numbers.

51   56   60

4. Write the numbers by fives to 60.
   Circle the tens.

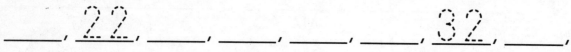

___5___, ___10___, _____, _____, _____, _____, _____, _____, _____,

_____, _____, ___60___

Even That Is Odd

1. Write the missing numbers on the number lines.

6 1 _ _ _ _ _ _ _ _ 7 0

2. Write the even numbers.

5 2 , ___ , 5 6 , ___ , 6 0

6 2 , ___ , ___ , ___ , ___

4 2 , ___ , ___ , ___ , 5 0

7 1 _ _ _ _ _ _ _ _ 8 0

3. Write the odd numbers.

5 1 , ___ , 5 5 , ___ , ___ , 6 1

7 1 , ___ , ___ , 7 7 , ___ , 8 1

6 1 , ___ , ___ , ___ , 6 9 , ___

What Grows on Trees?

1. Write the missing numbers.

2. Write the numbers before and after.

before	after		before	after
____	89	____	____	83	____
____	85	____		87	____

3. Write the missing numbers.

4. Write the numbers by tens to 100.

10, 20 ____, ____, ____, ____, ____, ____, ____, 100

5. Count backwards from 100–10 by tens.

100, ____, ____, ____, 60 ____, ____, ____, ____, ____

Name_____

Hundreds Chart

Write the missing numbers.

1	2				6			9	
11				15			18		
		23				27			
					36				40
				45					50
51					57				
	62					68			
		73			76				
81				85				89	
	92								100

Fancy Fives

1. Connect the numbers by fives.

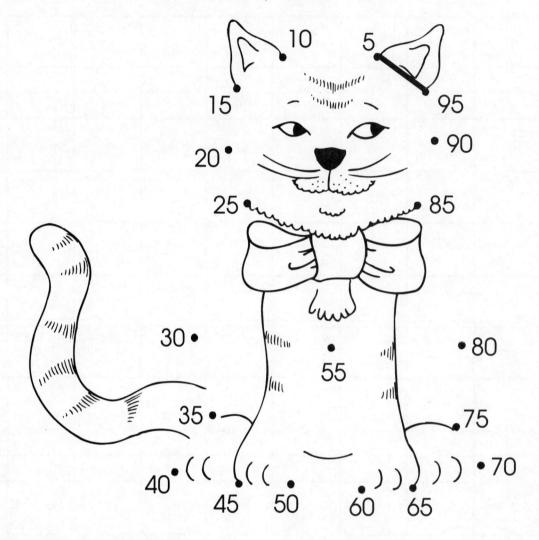

2. Write the numbers.

5 less	5 more	10 less	10 more
70	75		50
	60		90
	45		80

Super Tallies

A. Read the tally marks. Write the numbers.

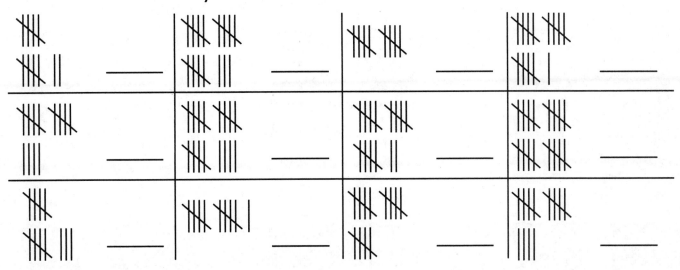

B. Count and tally.

C. Tally one more than . . .

15	~~IIII~~ ~~IIII~~ ~~IIII~~ I	12	
17		18	

FS-23201 Math Made Simple ▪ © Frank Schaffer Publications, Inc.

Above and Below

1. Color each bear with the bigger number.

2. Color each dog with the smallest number.

FS-23201 Math Made Simple ▪ © Frank Schaffer Publications, Inc.

Bubble Up

1. Write the missing numbers counting by twos.

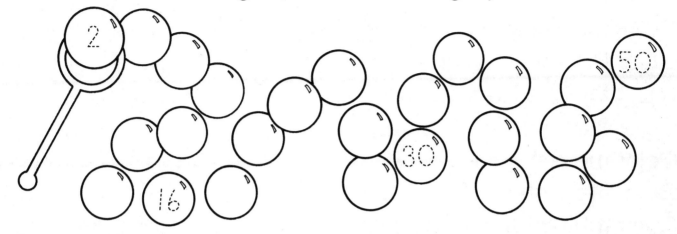

2. Write the missing numbers counting by fives.

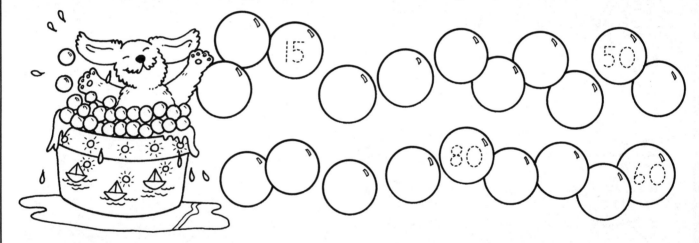

3. Write the missing numbers counting by tens.

Name_____

Who's First?

The ducks are in a race.

Color the second duck green.
Color the seventh duck red.
Color the fifth duck brown.
Color the tenth duck purple.
Color the first duck yellow.
Color the sixth duck black.
Color the ninth duck blue.
Color the third duck orange.
Color the eighth duck pink.
Color the fourth duck gray.

FS-23201 Math Made Simple • © Frank Schaffer Publications, Inc.

Addition and Subtraction

This section contains wonderful activities to help students develop an understanding of addition and subtraction through the use of concrete materials. Students will use symbols to add and subtract large numbers as appropriate to their levels of thinking. They should also use their understanding of fact families to help them see the relationship between addition and subtraction. The use of estimation skills should help students determine if the answers they arrive at are logical.

CONCEPTS

The ideas and activities presented in this section will help students explore the following concepts:

- *doubles*
- *fact families*
- *addition to 18*
- *2-digit addition (no regrouping)*
- *subtraction through 18*
- *2-digit subtraction (no regrouping)*
- *problem solving*

WHAT SCHOOL DAY IS TODAY?

Class Activity

Each day when you do your daily calendar activities, have the students count the days of school that have already been completed. At first, the students will be counting forward. Within a short while, they will be counting forward and backward. You can begin to ask them such questions as "If we add one more day to this month, how many days will it have?" or "If we took away one day from this month, how many days would it have?" You could also introduce the concept of zero, explaining to the students that this creates no change in the total. As the year goes on, students could advance to adding the digits in the day (for example, on day 24, they could add 2 + 4, etc.).

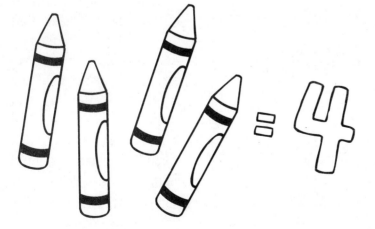

QUANTITY VERSUS NUMBERS

Manipulative Activity

Students need to understand that numbers represent quantities. Explain to them that the number 4 stands for 4 things, and its symbol is 4. Show the students 4 concrete things, then write the number 4, indicating that it stands for the 4 objects.

DOUBLES

Class Activity

A good place to begin teaching addition and subtraction is with doubles. Use dominoes or linking cubes to show 2 + 2, 3 + 3, etc. Have students discover things that come in pairs, or twos (eyes, ears, feet, shoes, socks, etc.). Make a class big book. Begin with things that come in twos. Then, every few days, add a new page that features a new number. For example, to depict things that come in threes, students could draw triplets, tricycle wheels, etc. On each page, write the doubles fact (2 + 2 = 4, 3 + 3 = 6, etc.) and talk about two sets of eyes, two pairs of shoes, etc.

Variation: As students become familiar with the doubles facts, you can add questions such as "If two and two make four, what will two and three make?" This will extend students' thinking to one more.

Class Demonstration

Headband
Adding/**S**ubtracting **A**ctivity

Make headbands for the students. One half of the students each need a headband with a red bird. The other half each need a headband with a blue bird. Make problems related to number facts by adding several students with headbands or subtracting several students with headbands. For example, 4 red birds and 2 blue birds make how many birds? (Have 4 students with red bird headbands and 2 with blue bird headbands come to the front of the class. Then have the seated students count the total number of students standing at the front of the class.) Or, if there are 6 birds and 2 flew away, how many birds are left? (Have 6 students with any colors of headbands come to the front of the class. Then have 2 students sit down. Seated students count how many students are left standing.)

DICE ROLL

Game

Divide the students into small groups. Give each group 20 counters and two dice. Each student in the small group takes a turn by rolling the dice and adding the two numbers together. After each student has had a turn, the student with the largest sum gets to take one of the counters. Each student then tosses the dice again. Play continues until all counters are claimed or when a certain amount of time has elapsed.

FS-23201 Math Made Simple ■ © Frank Schaffer Publications, Inc.

FACT FAMILIES

Manipulative Activity

Using two colors of linking cubes, you can begin to teach addition and subtraction facts by families. Use the cubes to show that 2 + 3 is the same as 3 + 2. Students can flip their linking cubes over, showing this concept concretely. They can also see that by taking away 2, there are 3 left. In this section are practice pages (pages 28 and 34) you can use to introduce students to fact families. If you do not have cubes, students can get the idea by coloring sample cubes. Using cubes will reinforce the facts.

Note: Have students save their completed fact family pages for review, for homework, or for school-home communication.

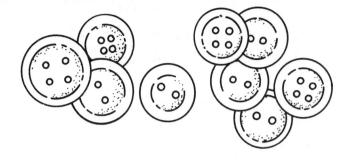

SHOW THE NUMBER

Manipulative Activity

Give each student 20 small objects (i.e., buttons) on his or her desk. On the board, write a number. The student should take that same number of objects and place them in a row. Write another number on the board. You can have students either add that number to the number of objects they already have, or you can have students subtract the number of objects. This manipulative activity really helps students understand the concepts of addition and subtraction.

PROBLEM-SOLVING STRATEGIES

Group Activity

Encourage students to make up and/or solve problems related to number facts as often as possible. Show them such techniques as guess and check; how to make a chart, a table, or a picture; how to find a pattern; etc. Draw examples on the board or on a chart. Have the students explain how they found the answers. See if anyone has another idea for finding the answers. For example, tell students that 8 inches of snow fell on Tuesday. Two more inches fell on Wednesday. Ask students how many inches of snow fell altogether. A good strategy to use to solve this problem would be to draw a picture showing 8 inches, then 2 more, for a total of 10 inches.

2 inches
8 inches

Homework

School-Home Connection

Encourage parents to have children add and subtract things at home, and to solve such simple problems as, "If we have 3 forks, how many more will we need so that we can give one to each person eating dinner with us?," or "I had 6 cups on the table, but Tommy just took one. How many are on the table now?"

Jumping Around

Add or subtract. Use the number line.

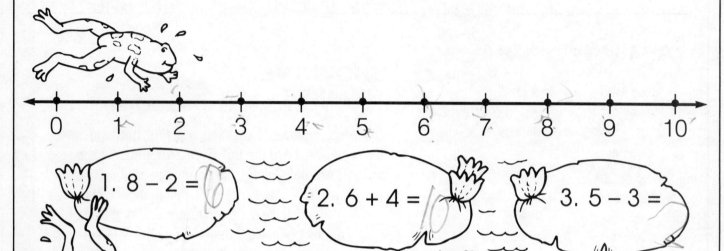

0 1 2 3 4 5 6 7 8 9 10

1. $8 - 2 =$ 6

2. $6 + 4 =$ 10

3. $5 - 3 =$

4. $6 - 4 =$ 2

5. $3 + 7 =$ 10

6. $4 + 5 =$ 9

7. $10 - 8 =$ 2

8. $5 + 2 =$ 7

9. $3 + 5 =$ 8

10. $9 - 7 =$ 2

11. $10 - 5 =$

12. $7 - 1 =$ 6

13. $1 + 8 =$ 9

14. $9 + 1 =$ 10

Party Time

Write the number sentences. Solve the problems.

A. 4 s at the party

4 s at the party

How many children?

_____ + _____ = _____

B. 5 s

Add 2 s.

How many in all?

_____ + _____ = _____

C. 8 s

3 s were eaten.

How many left?

_____ − _____ = _____

D. 8 s

7 s were opened.

How many left?

_____ − _____ = _____

E. 5 s

3 more s

How many in all?

_____ + _____ = _____

F. 2 s

3 more s

How many in all?

_____ + _____ = _____

Domino Delight

Write an addition sentence for each.

A.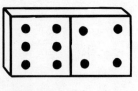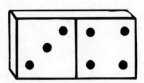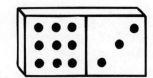

6 + 4 = 10

B.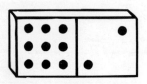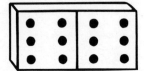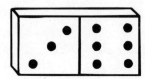

C.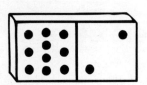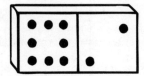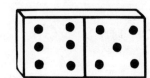

D.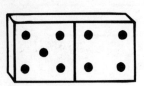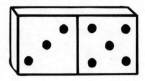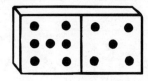

E.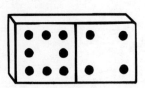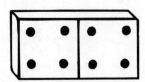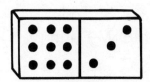

Fishing Fun

Subtract.

1. 12 − 8 =

2. 9 − 3 =

3. 7 − 1 =

4. 11 − 7 =

5. 12 − 10 =

6. 11 − 8 =

7. 10 − 6 =

8. 8 − 5 =

9. 9 − 7 =

10. 10 − 2 =

11. 12 − 6 =

All in the Family

Write the fact families.

A. 6, 5, 11

6 + 5 = 11
5 + 6 = 11
11 - 6 = 5
11 - 5 = 6

4, 5, 9

3, 9, 12

B. 4, 6, 10

3, 8, 11

3, 5, 8

C. 3, 4, 7

2, 8, 10

5, 7, 12

Doubles and More

Think, write, and draw.

A.

1 + 1 = _2_   so 1 + 2 = _3_   3 − 2 = ____

B.

2 + 2 = ____   so 2 + 3 = ____   5 − 3 = ____

C.

3 + 3 = ____   so 3 + 4 = ____   7 − 4 = ____

D.

```
   4   so    4       9              5   so    5      11
 + 4      + 5     − 5            + 5      + 6     − 6
 ____     ____    ____           ____     ____    ____
```

E.

```
   7   so    7      15              9   so    9      19
 + 7      + 8     − 8            + 9      + 10    − 9
 ____     ____    ____           ____     ____    ____
```

Springtime

Solve and color:

6 = yellow   7, 8, 9 = red   10, 11, 12 = blue

13, 14, 15 = purple   16, 17 = orange

18, 19, 20 = green

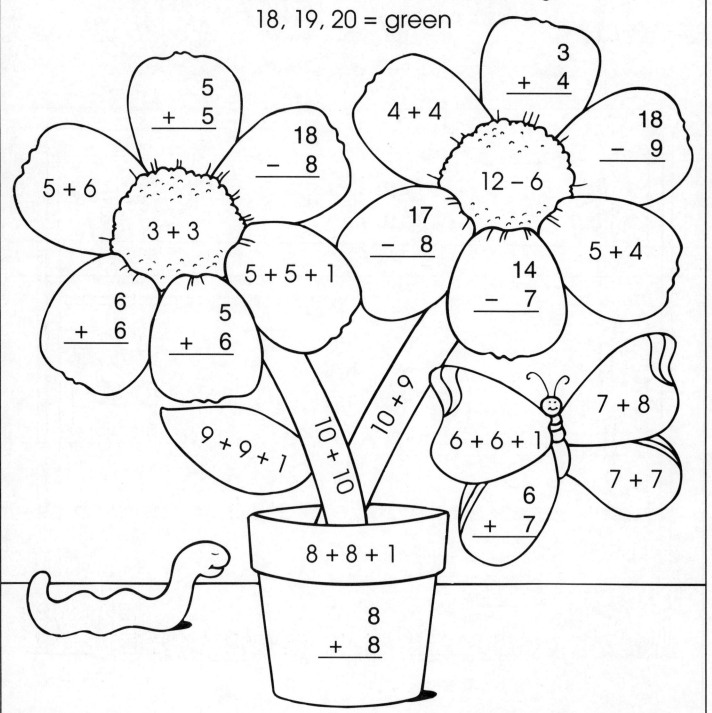

Mouse House

Add.

1. 5 + 6 =

2. 12 + 4 =

3. 10 + 8 =

4. 9 + 3 =

5. 8 + 2 =

6. 11 + 7 =

7. 10 + 6 =

8. 7 + 5 =

9. 8 + 7 =

Name_____

Critter Gritters

Subtract.

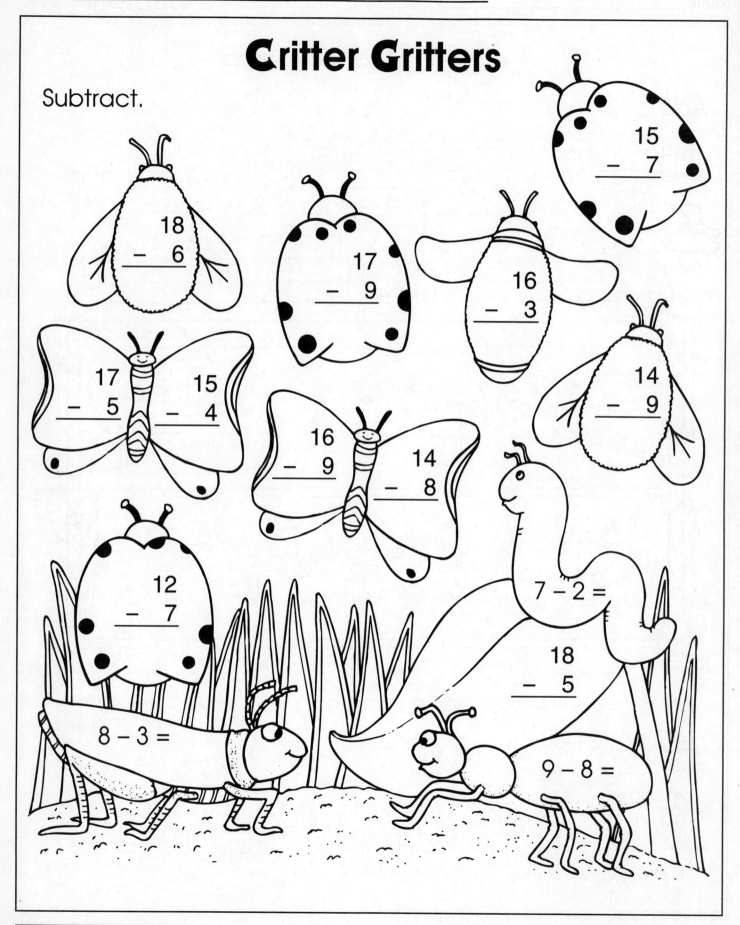

$$\begin{array}{r} 15 \\ -7 \\ \hline \end{array}$$

$$\begin{array}{r} 18 \\ -6 \\ \hline \end{array}$$

$$\begin{array}{r} 17 \\ -9 \\ \hline \end{array}$$

$$\begin{array}{r} 16 \\ -3 \\ \hline \end{array}$$

$$\begin{array}{r} 17 \\ -5 \\ \hline \end{array}$$

$$\begin{array}{r} 15 \\ -4 \\ \hline \end{array}$$

$$\begin{array}{r} 14 \\ -9 \\ \hline \end{array}$$

$$\begin{array}{r} 16 \\ -9 \\ \hline \end{array}$$

$$\begin{array}{r} 14 \\ -8 \\ \hline \end{array}$$

$$\begin{array}{r} 12 \\ -7 \\ \hline \end{array}$$

$7 - 2 =$

$$\begin{array}{r} 18 \\ -5 \\ \hline \end{array}$$

$8 - 3 =$

$9 - 8 =$

FS-23201 Math Made Simple ▪ © Frank Schaffer Publications, Inc.

Lead Me Home

Add or subtract.

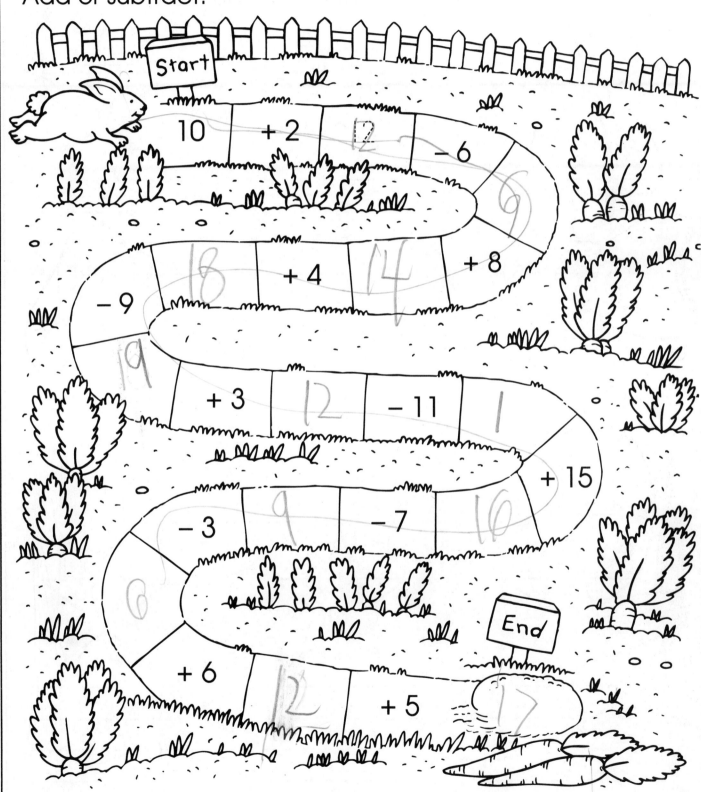

10   + 2   12   − 6   (9)

18   + 4   14   + 8

− 9   (19)

+ 3   12   − 11   1   + 15   (16)

− 3   9   − 7   (6)

+ 6   12   + 5   (17)

Start

End

Star Families

Write fact families. Use the numbers in the stars.

A.

7 + 8 = 15
8 + 7 = 15
15 − 7 = 8
15 − 8 = 7

B.

C.

FS-23201 Math Made Simple ▪ © Frank Schaffer Publications, Inc.

At the Beach

Write the number sentences. Solve the problems.

1. Sarah found 12 sand dollars.

   She gave away 3.

   How many are left?

   12
   − 3
   9

   ____12____ − ____3____ = ____9____

2. Tony saw 14 crabs.

   Three crabs ran away.

   How many crabs are left?

   14
   − 3
   11

   ____14____ − ____3____ = ____11____

3. Allison found 15 mussels.

   Three were open.

   How many were closed?

   15
   − 3
   12

   ____15____ − ____3____ = ____12____

4. There were 18 starfish on the beach.

   Ten got washed away.

   How many were left?

   18
   − 10
   8

   ____18____ − ____10____ = ____8____

5. In the shop, Mary bought these shells: _____

   5 wavy tops
   4 periwinkles
   6 clams

   How many shells did she buy?

   6
   4
   + 5

   ____6____ + ____4____ + ____5____ = ____15____

6. Bryan built 4 sandcastles.

   James built 2 sandcastles.

   John built 5 sandcastles.

   How many in all?

   4
   5
   +

   ____5____ + ____4____ + ____2____ = ____11____

Teddy Bear Sums

Add.

tens	ones
3	3
+	4
3	7

→

T | O
3 | 3
+ | 4
3 | 7

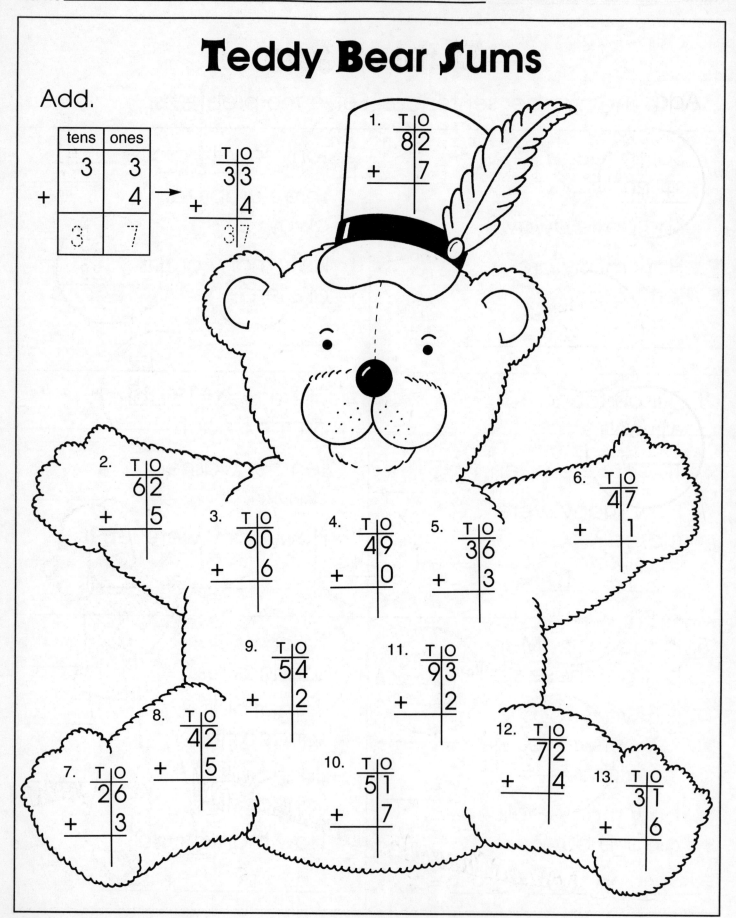

1.
T	O
8	2
+	7

2.
T	O
6	2
+	5

3.
T	O
6	0
+	6

4.
T	O
4	9
+	0

5.
T	O
3	6
+	3

6.
T	O
4	7
+	1

7.
T	O
2	6
+	3

8.
T	O
4	2
+	5

9.
T	O
5	4
+	2

10.
T	O
5	1
+	7

11.
T	O
9	3
+	2

12.
T	O
7	2
+	4

13.
T	O
3	1
+	6

Bubble Fun

Add.

$$\begin{array}{r} 19 \\ + 30 \\ \hline \end{array}$$

$$\begin{array}{r} 43 \\ + 32 \\ \hline \end{array}$$

$$\begin{array}{r} 22 \\ + 61 \\ \hline \end{array}$$

tens	ones
3	2
+ 4	1
7	3

$$\rightarrow \begin{array}{r} 32 \\ + 41 \\ \hline 73 \end{array}$$

$$\begin{array}{r} 72 \\ + 25 \\ \hline \end{array}$$

$$\begin{array}{r} 35 \\ + 33 \\ \hline \end{array}$$

$$\begin{array}{r} 36 \\ + 13 \\ \hline \end{array}$$

$$\begin{array}{r} 26 \\ + 41 \\ \hline \end{array}$$

$$\begin{array}{r} 40 \\ + 29 \\ \hline \end{array}$$

$$\begin{array}{r} 82 \\ + 15 \\ \hline \end{array}$$

$$\begin{array}{r} 48 \\ + 11 \\ \hline \end{array}$$

$$\begin{array}{r} 56 \\ + 42 \\ \hline \end{array}$$

$$\begin{array}{r} 83 \\ + 14 \\ \hline \end{array}$$

$$\begin{array}{r} 37 \\ + 30 \\ \hline \end{array}$$

$$\begin{array}{r} 24 \\ + 72 \\ \hline \end{array}$$

$$\begin{array}{r} 61 \\ + 25 \\ \hline \end{array}$$

$$\begin{array}{r} 47 \\ + 12 \\ \hline \end{array}$$

Name _____

Snowflake Fun

Subtract.

	tens	ones	
	8	6	86
–	1	3	→ – 13
	7	3	73

29
– 18

97
– 23

86
– 73

64
– 23

72
– 40

89
– 75

29
– 17

66
– 24

55
– 32

73
– 51

97
– 75

59
– 18

Beautiful Butterflies

Subtract.

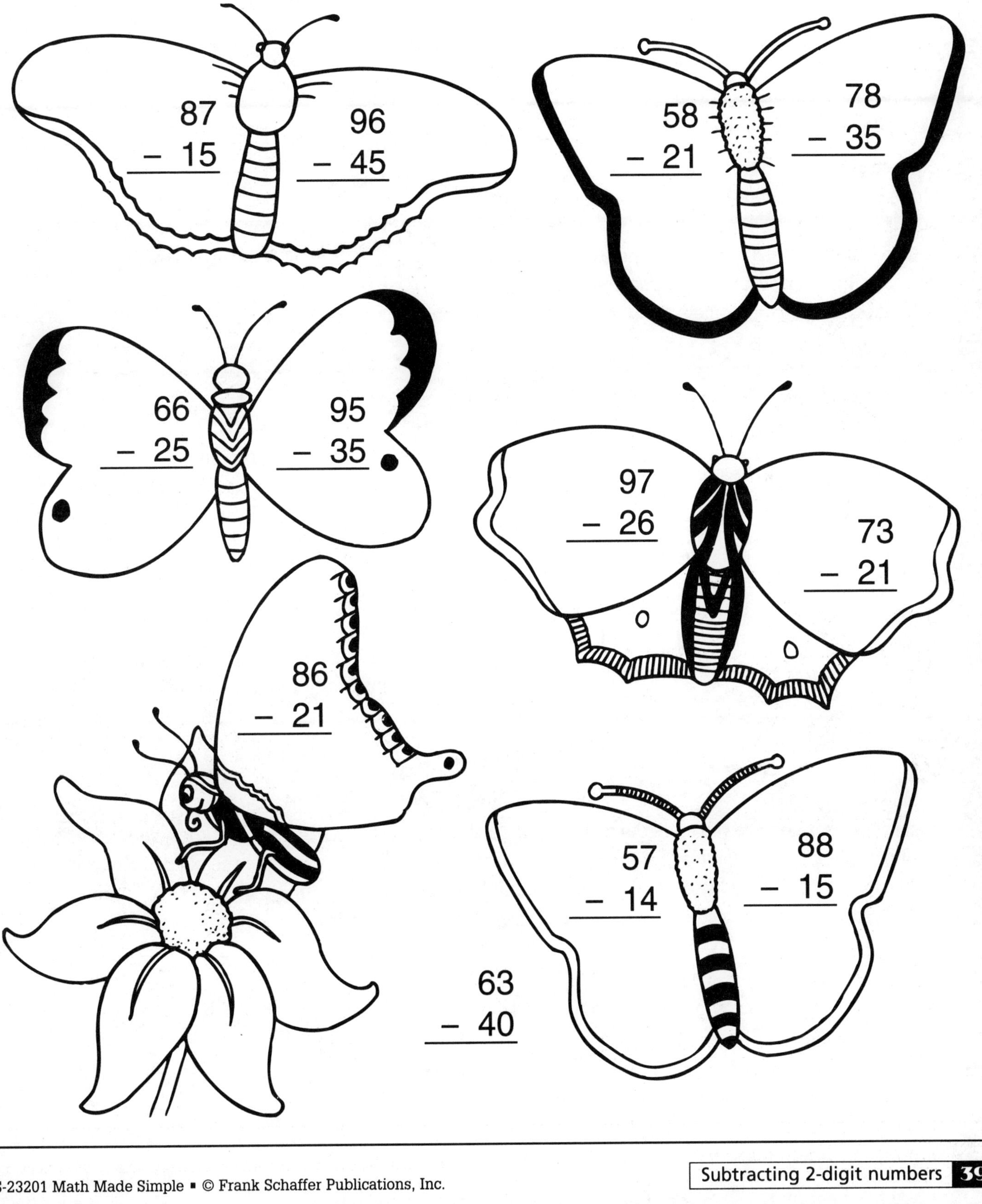

87
− 15

96
− 45

58
− 21

78
− 35

66
− 25

95
− 35

97
− 26

73
− 21

86
− 21

57
− 14

88
− 15

63
− 40

G ometry, M asurement, and Fractions

With the help of the activities in this section, students can manipulate models of shapes and solids to develop an understanding of their properties and spatial relationships. The experiences students do now will provide a more solid background for more advanced geometry presented in future years.

Measurements and fractions are used in daily life to help people understand, organize, and compare objects and materials found in their environments. Many hands-on opportunities for measuring and learning about fractions must be provided for students to help them understand these important concepts.

CONCEPTS

The ideas and activities presented in this section will help students explore the following concepts:

- circles, triangles, squares, rectangles
- measuring with rulers (centimeters and inches)
- liters/cups
- kilograms/pounds
- ½, ⅓, ¼

DRAWING SHAPES

Class Activity

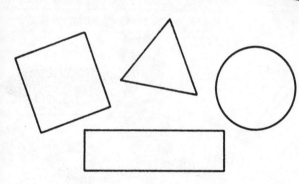

Draw basic shapes (circle, triangle, square, rectangle) on the board. Have the students practice drawing them at their desks. While the students are drawing the shapes, talk about the different aspects of each one. Count the sides, corners, and angles of the shapes. Talk about which shapes have no sides. Then have the students draw shape pictures. They can make a chart showing all the shapes they used and the number of them they used in their pictures.

USING GEOBOARDS

Manipulative Activity

Using geoboards, have the students make basic shapes. They can make larger triangles, squares, etc., by moving the bands. To learn about area, have students count the squares inside the shapes. To learn about perimeter, have the students count the units around the outside edges of the shapes. Give students geoboard dot pages to record the shapes they make with the geoboards.

PICTURE CARDS

Center Activity

Make cards showing fractions (½, ⅓, ¼, and 1 whole) and cards with pictures showing the fractions. (Include ⅛ when students are ready.) Mark the back of each card with a color for self-checking. Put the cards in a center for students to practice matching.

MAKING NEW SHAPES FROM OLD ONES

Manipulative Activity

Using several of one shape, students can create new shapes. For example, two triangles can make a square, four small squares or rectangles can make a larger rectangle, etc. Then have the students use all different shapes to make new shapes. For example, a star can be created from a square and four triangles.

PARTS OF GROUPS AS FRACTIONS

Learning Activity

It is often harder for students to see part of a group as representing a fraction. Have them practice with a collection of objects such as buttons. Start with small groups of objects—for example, 2 buttons. Explain that each button is half of the whole group of two buttons. With four objects, help them understand that it takes two objects to make a half of a group. Students can advance to larger numbers, dividing them into two equal groups when they are ready.

FOLDING PAPER

Manipulative Activity

As a group activity, have students fold sheets of paper into halves, then again into fourths, then eighths, etc. Show students how a square can be folded diagonally into two triangles. Let students make other discoveries about the different ways to get equal parts by folding. Point out, too, that some shapes they fold will not be equal. Have students label the parts they fold, such as ½, ¼, and ⅛, if they are ready for this step.

RULER FUN

Manipulative Activity

As young students learn to use a ruler, they need to be shown that they must start measuring from the end of the ruler, not the first number. Demonstrate carefully how to measure. Show the students how to line up their rulers with what they are measuring. The end of the ruler must line up with the dot, the end of the line, or the end of the object to be measured. Provide a lot of opportunities for students to measure things.

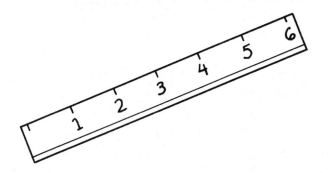

Learning Activity

Using Solid Shapes

When the students are familiar with the basic shapes, start introducing solid shapes such as the sphere, pyramid, cylinder, cube, cone, and rectangular prism. Display examples of these shapes for the students to see. Have them look around the classroom and at home for the many ways the shapes are used. Make a chart showing uses of the shapes (cans, balls, ice cream cones, etc.).

FS-23201 Math Made Simple ■ © Frank Schaffer Publications, Inc.

MEASURING WITH UNITS

Manipulative Activity

Have students practice measuring using things other than rulers. For example, they could use jumbo paper clips. Have the students estimate how many clips (units) it will take to measure a pencil. Then have the students work in small groups to place paper clips end to end to actually measure the pencil. Repeat with other units and objects to measure.

For more fun, have the students estimate how many more units it will take if they measure two crayons instead of one, etc.

OTHER TYPES OF MEASUREMENT

Learning Activities

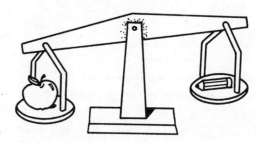

- Measuring in first grade should include using a balance scale to compare weights. Students can estimate how many plastic bears it will take to balance another object such as a board eraser. Students will find all kinds of objects in the room to weigh and compare.

- If you have a scale, students can measure in grams and kilograms and in ounces and pounds. Students can begin by estimating the weight of certain objects. Then they can place the items on the scale to weigh them.

- Have students bring, or provide a variety of, containers they can use to pour and compare liquids. They can estimate which containers will hold more than a given amount and which will hold less. Then they can pour water into the containers to check their estimates. At home, they can help or watch their parents measure ingredients for cooking.

Homework

School-Home Connection

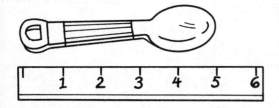

Scavenger Hunt

Send home letters to parents having them ask their children to look around their homes for a variety of shapes. Together, they should make a list of all the shapes they see. Compile the children's lists to make a class chart of the shapes they found. A few examples include doors, windows, stop signs, etc.

Measuring Mania

In letters sent home, encourage parents to let their children practice measuring. Children can measure such things as toothbrushes, spoons, etc. Have the children make lists of things to measure. Tell parents to help their children make charts showing such things as the sizes of shoes of family members, the lengths of people's hair, etc.

FS-23201 Math Made Simple ▪ © Frank Schaffer Publications, Inc.

Get in Shape

Match.

triangle

circle

square

rectangle

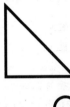

Draw 3 different circles. Color them.	Draw 4 different triangles. Color them.
Draw 2 different rectangles. Color them.	Draw 5 different squares. Color them.

How Many?

Color △ blue, ▢ red, ○ green, and ▭ yellow.

Count the shapes.

A.

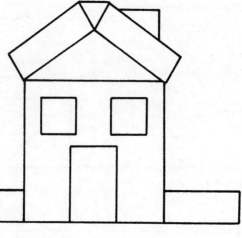

How many?

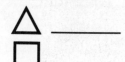

B.

How many?

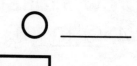

C.

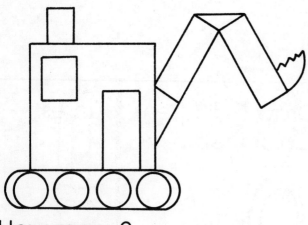

How many?

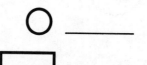

D.

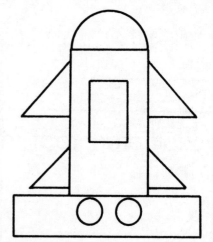

How many?

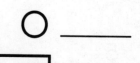

FS-23201 Math Made Simple • © Frank Schaffer Publications, Inc.

Let's Measure

Use a ruler. Measure the objects.

How wide is it?

1. _____ cm

2. _____ cm

3. _____ cm

4. _____ cm

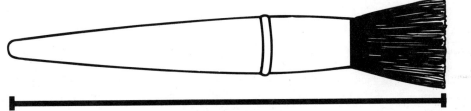

How tall is it?

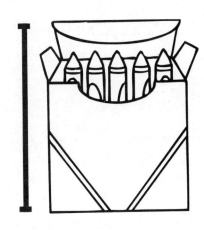

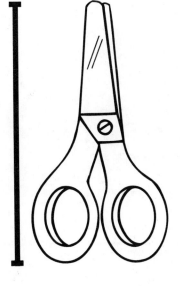

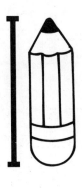

5. _____ cm   6. _____ cm   7. _____ cm

How Far?

How far did Tommy Turtle travel? Use a ruler to measure how many inches.

1. _____

_____ inches

2. _____

_____ inches

3. _____

_____ inches

4. _____

_____ inches

5. _____

_____ inches

6. _____

_____ inches

How Much Is Too Much?

less than a liter   **1 liter**   **more than a liter**

Draw a circle around things that hold more than a liter.

Draw an X on things that hold less than a liter.

Each liter has 4 cups. Color the number of cups to show each amount.

Weight a Minute!

A. How many kilograms?

___ kilograms   ___ kilograms   ___ kilograms

B. Circle things that weigh less than a kilogram.

   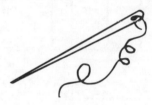

C. How many pounds?

___ pounds   ___ pounds   ___ pounds

D. Circle things that weigh more than a pound.

FS-23201 Math Made Simple ■ © Frank Schaffer Publications, Inc.

How Many Parts?

Write how many equal parts. Color each a different color.

A. 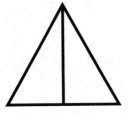   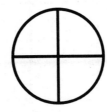   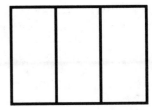

_____ parts   _____ parts   _____ parts

B. 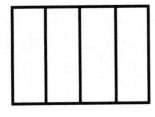   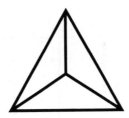   

_____ parts   _____ parts   _____ parts

C. Draw lines to make two equal parts.

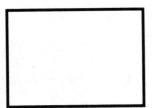   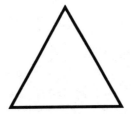   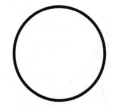

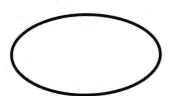      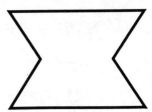

High Flyers

A. Color and write $\frac{1}{2}$.

 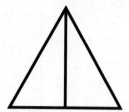 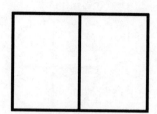

_____   _____   _____

C. Color and write $\frac{1}{4}$.

_____

B. Color and write $\frac{1}{3}$.

 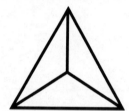 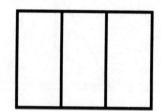 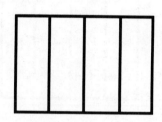

_____   _____   _____   _____

D. Color one part of each kite. Write the fraction.

FS-23201 Math Made Simple • © Frank Schaffer Publications, Inc.

Money

The activities in this section are a great way to help students learn the relative value of coins as they use them in real-life problem solving situations. Experiences in counting by ones, fives, and tens also help students evaluate sets of coins.

CONCEPTS

The ideas and activities presented in this section will help students explore the following concepts:

- *pennies*
- *nickels*
- *dimes*
- *quarters*
- *comparing money*
- *making change*
- *critical thinking*

STUDENT KITS — Manipulative Activity

Before starting the activities in this section, make each student a kit. In the kit, include pennies, nickels, dimes, and quarters of play or paper money. If using paper money, you might want to cut a box around the coin and copy the coins on heavy stock paper. They will last longer this way. Whenever possible, have students practice using real money.

COUNTING EXPERIENCES — Class Activity

Frequently, provide short periods during which the students count money. Have them count by pennies (ones) to a given amount such as 20. Or, they can count by nickels (fives) to 25. Introduce the idea of 5 pennies being equal to one nickel, 10 pennies being equal to a dime, 5 nickels being equal to a quarter, etc. Students can also count by dimes (tens) to 100 or more, noting that 10 dimes are equal to one dollar.

FUNNY MONEY — Class Activity

In addition to counting, have students show various amounts of money on their desks using their student kits. They can add different amounts and find totals. Eventually, you can transfer to mental math skills by asking students to add 4 cents and 8 cents without using manipulatives. Have students show their answers to you on their erasable cards.

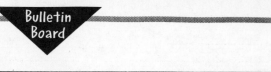

Coin Presidents

Copy and enlarge or purchase pictures of the heads and tails sides of coins. Create a bulletin board depicting both sides of coins. Teach students what objects or symbols appear on coins. Have students learn that Lincoln is on the head's side of a penny and that the Lincoln Memorial is on the tail's side. (This could be a great tie-in with Social Studies/History.) Note that Jefferson and Monticello are on the nickel, F. D. Roosevelt and a torch are on the dime, and Washington and the American eagle are on the quarter. You may wish to proceed to bills if the class shows interest.

MONEY MATCHING

Learning Center

Put the two activities below at a center. Have students visit the center and complete the activities during free time.

- Cut out pictures of toy advertisements. Glue each one to a card. Attach or add price tags for the items on the cards. On other cards, show the amounts of the items in coins. Have the students match the coins with the items. Color-code the backs of the cards for self-checking.

- You could make another set of cards depicting coins and written amounts. For example, one card might depict three nickels, while another card depicts 15¢. As students become familiar with counting money, add larger and larger amounts.

USING REAL OBJECTS

Learning Center

Have students bring in small, non-valuable objects or toys, empty boxes, etc. Put price tags on all of the objects the students bring in. Set up a center or a store area in which students can buy, sell, make change, etc., using the objects. Using real objects adds interest when working with money.

Homework

SCHOOL-HOME CONNECTION

Ask parents to work with their children on counting money, exchanging equivalent amounts of small coins for a larger coin, etc. At the store, parents should have their children say how much items cost, compare prices, actually purchase items, etc.

Money Fun

You have 15¢. Write the number sentences.

How much change?

1.  5¢	15¢ – 5¢ = 10¢	10¢
2.  9¢	____¢ – ____¢ = ____¢	____¢
3.  6¢	____¢ – ____¢ = ____¢	____¢
4.  8¢	____¢ – ____¢ = ____¢	____¢
5. 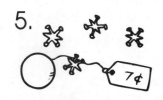 7¢	____¢ – ____¢ = ____¢	____¢
6.  10¢	____¢ – ____¢ = ____¢	____¢

7. Write the number sentence:

You have 20¢. You buy and . How much do you have left? _____¢ – _____¢ = _____¢

Missing Coins

Which coins are missing? Write them. Use ⒟ ⓝ ⓟ.
dime nickel penny

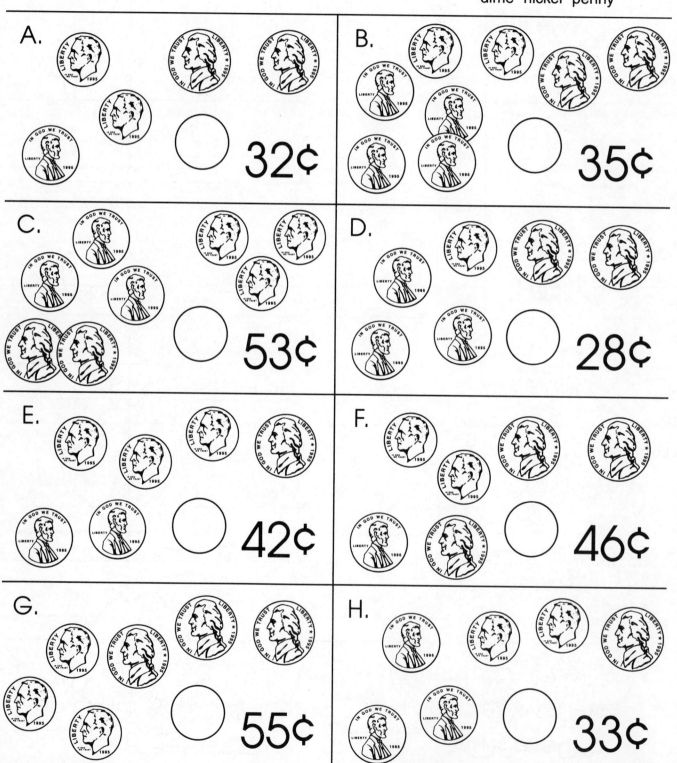

A.   ◯   32¢

B.   ◯   35¢

C.   ◯   53¢

D.   ◯   28¢

E.   ◯   42¢

F.   ◯   46¢

G.   ◯   55¢

H.   ◯   33¢

FS-23201 Math Made Simple • © Frank Schaffer Publications, Inc.

Count Amounts

Count. Write the amounts.

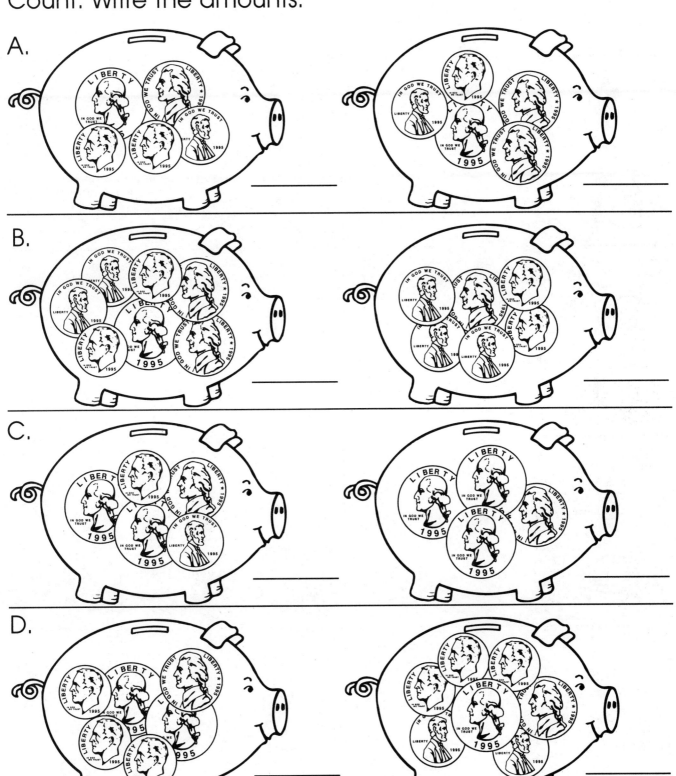

A.

B.

C.

D.

Quarters, dimes, nickels, and pennies **55**

Matching Money

Count. Match.

  • •

 • •

 • •

 • •

 • •

• •

FS-23201 Math Made Simple ▪ © Frank Schaffer Publications, Inc.

More Money

Circle the greater amount in each row.

A.

B.

C.

D.

E.

Go Shopping

Count. Can you buy the item? Circle **yes** or **no**.

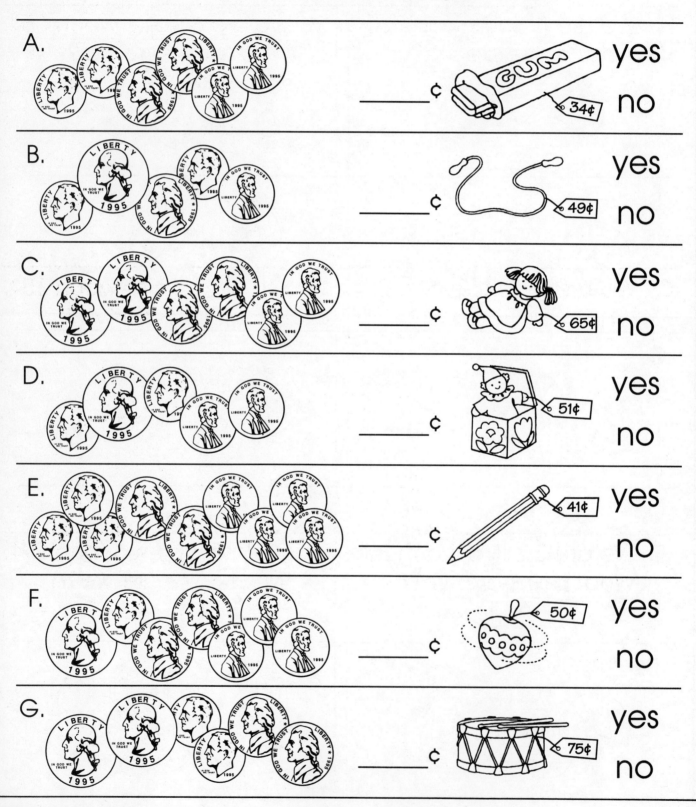

A. _____¢   GUM 34¢   yes   no

B. _____¢   49¢   yes   no

C. _____¢   65¢   yes   no

D. _____¢   51¢   yes   no

E. _____¢   41¢   yes   no

F. _____¢   50¢   yes   no

G. _____¢   75¢   yes   no

   FS-23201 Math Made Simple ■ © Frank Schaffer Publications, Inc.

Funny Money

Draw coins to solve each riddle.

A. We are 4 coins worth 30¢. What coins are we?

B. We are 6 coins worth 35¢. What coins are we?

C. We are 2 coins worth 26¢. What coins are we?

D. We are 3 coins worth 15¢. What coins are we?

E. We are 3 coins worth 35¢. What coins are we?

F. We are 5 coins worth 29¢. What coins are we?

Critical thinking **59**

Solve It

Add or subtract. Write how much.

A. had a .

Then she got a .

How much does she have now?

_____¢

B. had a .

Then he got .

How much does he have now?

_____¢

C. had a .

He spent .

How much does he have now?

_____¢

D. had a .

She spent a .

How much does she have now?

_____¢

E. had .

Then he got .

How much does he have now?

_____¢

F. had .

She spent a .

How much does she have now?

_____¢

FS-23201 Math Made Simple • © Frank Schaffer Publications, Inc.

Time

A class clock with movable hands, large enough for all of the students to see, is a good object to have when working with some of the activities in this section. A paper plate as a base and cardstock for hands can be used to make one, if necessary. For more individual practice, have each student make a clock to use, or purchase some clocks. Help the students write all or some of the numbers on the clocks. Students may be able to fill in any missing numbers, depending on their abilities. Or, you may wish to have the numbers all uniform. (In this case, have an adult write the numbers.) These clocks are also a great way for parents to work on time concepts with their children.

CONCEPTS

The ideas and activities presented in this section will help students explore the following concepts:
- **days of the week**
- **months of the year**
- **calendars**
- **seasons**
- **time to the hour**
- **time to the half-hour**
- **elapsed time**
- **a.m. and p.m.**

INTRODUCING THE CLOCK HANDS
Directed Activity

Review with the students the meaning of the "little hand" for the hour and the "big hand" for the minutes. Below is a little rhyme you may wish to use.

When the big hand is straight up,
The little hand the hour will tell.
Now it's eleven o'clock, yes, eleven o'clock,
Can you hear the bell?

Have a student ring a bell or a triangle, ringing one time for each hour. Have the children ring slowly as they count the hours aloud.

DAY TO DAY
Song

Teach the students a song about the days of the week to the tune of "Clementine."

There are 7 days, there are 7 days, there are 7 days in a week.
Sunday, Monday,
Tuesday, Wednesday,
Thursday, Friday, Saturday.

Is it Sunday? Is it Sunday? Is it Sunday? No it's not.
Is it Monday?
Yes, it's Monday.
It's the second day of the week.

Add verses, but always stop on the day of the week that you are singing about. Sing the song every day for a short while, then just occasionally.

MONTH-TO-MONTH

Song

When students are familiar with the days of the week, teach them the month song below to the tune of "London Bridge."

Let's say the months of the year, of the year, of the year,
Let's say the months of the year,
All together.

Then chant together the following: January (clap), February (snap or tap shoulders or other body part or desk), March (clap), April (tap), etc.

Gradually, you can add ordinal numbers such as "January, first month, February, second month," etc. Pretty soon, the students will add new ideas of their own.

SEASONS

Science Connection

Talk about the seasons with the students. Read a book such as *Sky Tree* by Locker (HarperCollins, 1995) or another of your choice. Discuss the changes in plants and weather as the seasons change. If you live in an area where the leaves change color, have the students bring leaves to school. Classifying leaves into categories by color or shape is a great math activity. You can introduce simple Venn diagrams by focusing on such aspects as color, size, and shape of leaves.

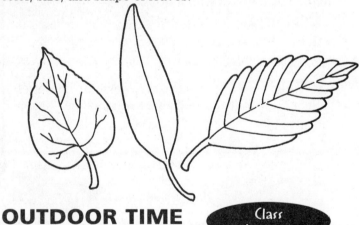

OUTDOOR TIME

Class Activity

Using paper plates numbered from 1–12, make a large clock on the playground. Make large clock hands from cardboard. Move the hands. Have the students tell the time by the hour, and later, by the half-hour. Students can take turns moving the hands for the group, or you can call out an hour, and students can take turns standing by that hour. When you are discussing half-hours, it will be easier for the students to see and feel that they must move part of the way toward the next hour. This is usually one of the hardest concepts to teach.

MONTHLY STUDENT CALENDARS

Class Activities

Each month, give students copies of blank calendars. Have the students fill in their calendars. Students can fill in their calendars by copying the class calendar. Be sure each student starts on the correct day of the month!

- When they are ready, students can note holidays, birthdays, or other special days using such symbols as candles or flags.

- You can also have students color calendars according to specific directions.

- When students are confident with the days of the week and the numbers on a calendar, begin to expand your calendar activities to include thinking questions such as "What day of the week is March 4th?", "What day will it be two days from now?", "What day will it be a week from now?"

- As an enrichment activity, have students work in pairs to think of calendar questions. Have them ask their questions and select students to answer the questions during calendar time.

NUMBER PATTERNS

Class Activity

Using your classroom calendar, point out the days of the week as you sing the song described in "Day to Day" (page 61). Then when the students are able, have a student point out the days. Next, point out the numbers of the days on the calendar. During the first month, use two kinds of cutouts, such as bears and suns. Place one type of cutout on all of the odd numbers, and the other one on the even numbers. This is an A-B pattern. Students will see the pattern, and they'll begin to recognize odd and even numbers. As the year progresses, make the patterns more difficult. For example, use chick, chick, rabbit (A-A-B).

A.M.—P.M.

Class Demonstration

Explain to the students how Earth revolves around the sun. Tell them that this is why we have seasons. To help the students understand this concept, have the students stand in a circle on the playground. Choose one student to stand in the center holding a sun. Have the students walk around the circle. Tell the students in the circle that they are Earth revolving around the sun.

Next, have the students turn around in place. Tell them that this indicates day and night. When they face the sun, it is daytime. At night, they face away from the sun. This is when the other side of the world, the part that is now facing the sun, has daytime.

Use the class clock to teach the students that 12 hours make up day, or a.m., time, and another 12 hours make up night, or p.m., time. Demonstrate that when the clock goes fully around each set of 12 hours completing 24 hours, one complete day has passed, and it is time to move to a new day on the calendar.

MATCH-UP

Game

On index cards, write different times using words or numbers and matching times on clocks. Put the cards in a center. Let the students go to the center and match the words with a clock that shows the time and vice-versa. Color-code the backs of the cards for self-checking.

Art Project

Making a Sundial

A sundial is a lot of fun for students to make. To make one, cut out a tagboard circle, write the clock numbers on it, but do not attach the hands. Make one for each student or for each small group of students. On a sunny day, take the clocks out onto the grass. Have an adult help the students stick pencils or dowels through the clocks' centers into the ground. Each hour, take the students out to check on the clocks. Have the students mark where the shadows are each time on the clocks. This activity will help them better understand Earth's rotation.

BEFORE AND AFTER

Pose the following to the students: "It's 9 o'clock. What time will it be in ___ hours?" (You can progress to half-hours when the students are ready.) Continue to play as long as the students are interested. Have them show the times on their clocks. As the year progresses, ask what time it will be in several hours or what time it was several hours before.

CLOCK PRACTICE

Individual Activity

Give the students plenty of opportunities to practice with their clocks. First lessons should have them moving just the little hand, keeping the big hand on 12. Later, they can place the big hand on 6 and practice placing the little hand just past the hour. Call out various hours or half-hours. Check for understanding. Keep emphasizing that the little hand shows the hours, and the big hand shows the minutes.

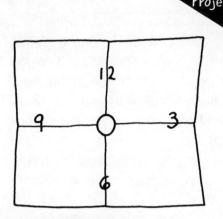

Art Project

LEARNING TO MAKE CLOCKS

For each student, cut a square of paper any size starting from about 6 inches up and getting bigger. Have the students fold their papers once each way, thus creating four sections. While folded, have the students use scissors to round off the folded point where all four corners meet. Tell them not to cut the other edges. After they open their papers, they each have a somewhat circular shape in the center of their papers. On the folds, have the students write the following hours in the correct positions: 3, 6, 9, 12. Last, have the students fill in the remaining missing numbers on the clocks.

Homework

School-Home Connection

There are many ways parents can help their children tell time. Suggest in the letters you send home that they help their children notice the many clocks there are at home, at school, and at public places. Parents can help their children notice the different types of clocks and the different ways there are to tell time. While doing different activities, have parents help children see what time they start an activity and what time they stop. (This can include going to bed, brushing teeth, playing games, working, etc.) All of these types of activities will help children better learn how to tell time.

In your letter to parents, suggest that they discuss days, weeks, and months with their children. Encourage parents to ask their children questions such as "What day of the week is it? What day will it be in two days?"

What's Next?

Trace the days.
Write the days in order.

Tuesday	1. <u>S</u>_____
Friday	2. _____
Sunday	3. _____
Wednesday	4. _____
Monday	5. _____
Thursday	6. _____
Saturday	7. _____

Write what day comes after Friday. _____

Ordering Days

Sunday	Monday	Tuesday	Wednesday	Thursday	Friday	Saturday
1st	2nd	3rd	4th	5th	6th	7th

Match.

1. Tuesday   1st

2. Sunday   2nd

3. Thursday   3rd

4. Monday   4th

5. Wednesday   5th

6. Saturday   6th

7. Friday   7th

8. The 7th day of the week is _____.

9. The 3rd day of the week is _____.

10. The 5th day of the week is _____.

11. What is your favorite day of the week? _____

FS-23201 Math Made Simple • © Frank Schaffer Publications, Inc.

Calendar Questions

May

Sunday	Monday	Tuesday	Wednesday	Thursday	Friday	Saturday
	1	2	3	4	5	6
7	8	9	10	11	12	13
14	15	16	17	18	19	20
21	22	23	24	25	26	27
28	29	30	31			

1. What is the name of this month? _____

2. How many days are in this month? _____

3. What day of the week is the 15th? _____

4. What is the date of the first Sunday? _____

5. What day is the first day of the month? _____

6. What is the date of the third Thursday? _____

7. How many Wednesdays are in this month? _____

8. Write the dates of all the Fridays in this month.

   _____

9. What day of the week does the next month begin on?

   _____

All Mixed Up

July   January   December   April
February   August   September   March
October   May   June   November

Write the months in order.

1. _____

2. _____

3. _____

4. _____

5. _____

6. _____

7. _____

8. _____

9. _____

10. _____

11. _____

12. _____

Write the month your birthday is in. _____

FS-23201 Math Made Simple ▪ © Frank Schaffer Publications, Inc.

Time for Time

Write the times.

1.

[:]

2.

[:]

3.

[:]

4.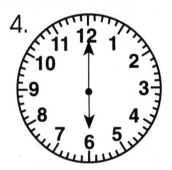

[:]

5.

[:]

6.

[:]

7.

[:]

8.

[:]

9.

[:]

Watch Out!

Match the correct times.

What Time Is It?

Match.

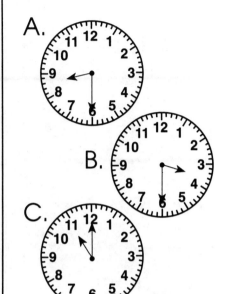

A.

B.

C.

D.

E.

F.

G.

H.

twelve o'clock

nine o'clock

three-thirty

twelve-thirty

four o'clock

six-thirty

eight-thirty

eleven o'clock

 9:00

 4:00

 8:30

 12:00

 6:30

 3:30

 11:00

12:30

My Day

Draw hands to show when you do each thing.

1.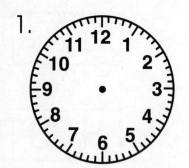

I wake up at
_____ o'clock.

2.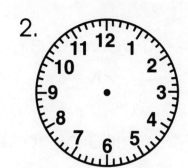

I eat breakfast at
_____ o'clock.

3.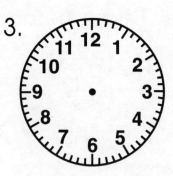

I go to school at
_____ o'clock.

4.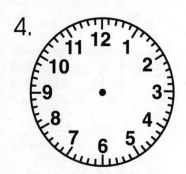

Recess is at
_____ o'clock.

5.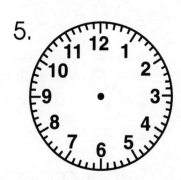

Lunch is at
_____ o'clock.

6.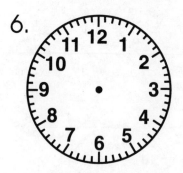

I go home at
_____ o'clock.

7.

I play with friends
at _____ o'clock.

8.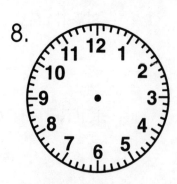

Dinner is at
_____ o'clock.

9.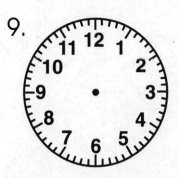

I go to bed at
_____ o'clock.

Before and After

Draw the hands. Write the times.

1 hour before   **1 hour after**

1.

_____   3:00   _____

2.

_____   _____   _____

3.

_____   _____   _____

4.

_____   _____   _____

Tricky Timing

Draw the hands. Write the times.

| **one-half hour earlier** | **one-half hour later** |

1. Before   Now

_____   _____

4. Now   Later

_____   _____

2. Before   Now

_____   _____

5. Now   Later

_____   _____

3. Before   Now

_____   _____

6. Now   Later

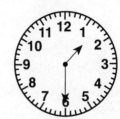 

_____   _____

FS-23201 Math Made Simple ▪ © Frank Schaffer Publications, Inc.

What's Next?

Write the times. Tell how long.

1. Sean started soccer practice at 4:00.

Practice ended at 6:00.

Practice lasted _____ hour(s).

2. Emily started her homework at 7:00.

She finished at 8:00.

How long did it take?

_____ hour(s)

3. The show started at 8:00.

Tim watched TV for one-half hour.

What time did the show end?

_____

4. Tracy read her book for one hour. She started reading at 6:30. What time did she finish? _____

Page 6

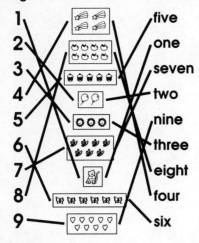

1 — five
2 — one
3 — seven
4 — two
5 — nine
6 — three
7 — eight
8 — four
9 — six

Page 7

A. 2, 10, 4, 8, 6

B. 2, 0, 8, 4, 6

C. 10, 9, 8, 7, 6, 5, 4, 3, 2, 1, 0

Page 8

A. 5, 8, 0; 7, 6, 9; 9, 3, 6

B. 10, 9, 8, 7, 6, 5, 4, 3, 2, 1, 0

C. Students should draw the number of items indicated.

Page 9

1. 2, 4, 6, 8, 10

2. 1, 3, 5, 7, 9

3. 2, 4, 6, 8, 10

4. 1, 3, 5, 7, 9

5. odd, even, odd, odd, even; even, even, even, odd, odd

Page 10

A. 12, 14; 14, 16; 16, 18; 11, 13; 17, 19

B. 10, 12; 13, 15; 18, 20; 15, 17; 9, 11

C. 20, 19, 18, 17, 16, 15, 14, 13, 12, 11, 10, 9, 8, 7, 6, 5, 4, 3, 2, 1, 0

Page 11

1. 21, 22, 23, 24, 25, 26, 27, 28, 29, 30

2. 25, 27; 21, 23; 28, 30

3. 31, 32, 33, 34, 35, 36, 37, 38, 39, 40

4. 35, 37; 31, 33; 36, 38; 38, 40

Page 12

1. 41, 42, 43, 44, 45, 46, 47, 48, 49, 50

2. 2, 4, 6, 8, 10, 12, 14, 16, 18, 20, 22, 24, 26, 28, 30, 32, 34, 36, 38, 40, 42, 44, 46, 48, 50

3. 51, 52, 53, 54, 55, 56, 57, 68, 59, 60

4. 5, 10, 15, 20, 25, 30, 35, 40, 45, 50, 55, 60

Page 13

1. 61, 62, 63, 64, 65, 66, 67, 68, 69, 70

2. 52, 54, 56, 58, 60; 62, 64, 66, 68, 70; 42, 44, 46, 48, 50; 71, 72, 73, 74, 75, 76, 77, 78, 79, 80

3. 51, 53, 55, 57, 59, 61; 71, 73, 75, 77, 79, 81; 61, 63, 65, 67, 69, 71

Page 14

1. 81, 82, 83, 84, 85, 86, 87, 88, 89, 90

2. 88, 90; 84, 86; 82, 84; 86, 88

3. 91, 92, 93, 94, 95, 96, 97, 98, 99, 100

4. 10, 20, 30, 40, 50, 60, 70, 80, 90, 100

5. 100, 90, 80, 70, 60, 50, 40, 30, 20, 10

Page 15

1	2	3	4	5	6	7	8	9	10
11	12	13	14	15	16	17	18	19	20
21	22	23	24	25	26	27	28	29	30
31	32	33	34	35	36	37	38	39	40
41	42	43	44	45	46	47	48	49	50
51	52	53	54	55	56	57	58	59	60
61	62	63	64	65	66	67	68	69	70
71	72	73	74	75	76	77	78	79	80
81	82	83	84	85	86	87	88	89	90
91	92	93	94	95	96	97	98	99	100

Page 16

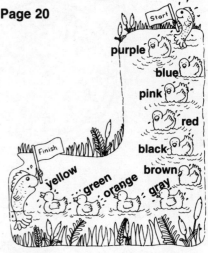

2. 70, 80; 55, 65; 40, 50; 40, 60; 80, 100; 70, 90

Page 17

A. 12, 18, 10, 16, 14, 19, 17, 20, 13, 11, 15, 14

B. 12, 15, 17, 20, 11, 14

C. ΗΗΙ ΗΗΙ III; ΗΗΙ ΗΗΙ ΗΗΙ III; ΗΗΙ ΗΗΙ ΗΗΙ IIII

Page 18

1. 70, 39, 44, 32, 61

2. 19, 30, 37, 89

Page 19

1. 2, 4, 6, 8, 10, 12, 14, 16, 18, 20, 22, 24, 26, 28, 30, 32, 34, 36, 38, 40, 42, 44, 46, 48, 50

2. 5, 10, 15, 20, 25, 30, 35, 40, 45, 50, 55, 60, 65, 70, 75, 80, 85, 90, 95, 100

3. 10, 20, 30, 40, 50, 60, 70, 80, 90, 100

Page 20

Start

purple
blue
pink
red
black
brown
yellow
green
orange
gray
Finish

Page 24

1. 6   2. 10   3. 2   4. 2

5. 10   6. 9   7. 2   8. 7

9. 8   10. 2   11. 5   12. 6

13. 9   14. 10

Page 25

A. 4 + 4 = 8   B. 5 + 2 = 7

C. 8 − 3 = 5   D. 8 − 7 = 1

E. 5 + 3 = 8   F. 2 + 3 = 5

Page 26

A. 6 + 4 = 10; 3 + 4 = 7; 9 + 3 = 12

B. 9 + 2 = 11; 6 + 6 = 12; 3 + 6 = 9

C. 10 + 2 = 12; 8 + 2 = 10; 6 + 5 = 11

D. 5 + 4 = 9; 3 + 5 = 8; 7 + 5 = 12

E. 8 + 4 = 12; 4 + 4 = 8; 9 + 3 = 12

Page 27

1. 4   2. 6   3. 6   4. 4

5. 2   6. 3   7. 4   8. 3

9. 2   10. 8   11. 6

FS-23201 Math Made Simple ▪ © Frank Schaffer Publications, Inc.

Page 28

A. 6 + 5 = 11, 5 + 6 = 11, 11 − 6 = 5, 11 − 5 = 6; 4 + 5 = 9, 5 + 4 = 9, 9 − 4 = 5, 9 − 5 = 4; 3 + 9 = 12, 9 + 3 = 12, 12 − 3 = 9, 12 − 9 = 3

B. 4 + 6 = 10, 6 + 4 = 10, 10 − 4 = 6, 10 − 6 = 4; 3 + 8 = 11, 8 + 3 = 11, 11 − 3 = 8, 11 − 8 = 3; 3 + 5 = 8, 5 + 3 = 8, 8 − 3 = 5, 8 − 5 = 3

C. 3 + 4 = 7, 4 + 3 = 7, 7 − 3 = 4, 7 − 4 = 3; 2 + 8 = 10, 8 + 2 = 10, 10 − 2 = 8, 10 − 8 = 2; 5 + 7 = 12, 7 + 5 = 12, 12 − 5 = 7, 12 − 7 = 5

Page 29

A. 2, 3, 1   B. 4, 5, 2   C. 6, 7, 3

D. 8, 9, 4; 10, 11, 5

E. 14, 15, 7; 18, 19, 10

Page 30

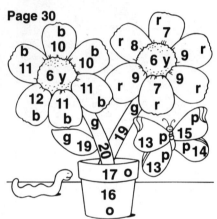

Page 31

1. 11   2. 16   3. 18
4. 12   5. 10   6. 18
7. 16   8. 12   9. 15

Page 32

Page 33

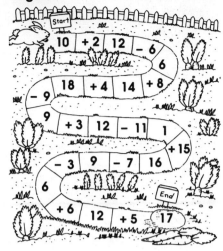

Page 34

A. 7 + 8 = 15, 8 + 7 = 15, 15 − 7 = 8, 15 − 8 = 7; 9 + 11 = 20, 11 + 9 = 20, 20 − 11 = 9, 20 − 9 = 11; 5 + 7 = 12, 7 + 5 = 12, 12 − 5 = 7, 12 − 7 = 5

B. 6 + 13 = 19, 13 + 6 = 19, 19 − 6 = 13; 19 − 13 = 6; 7 + 10 = 17, 10 + 7 = 17; 17 − 7 = 10, 17 − 10 = 7

C. 7 + 11 = 18, 11 + 7 = 18, 18 − 7 = 11, 18 − 11 = 7; 8 + 6 = 14, 6 + 8 = 14, 14 − 8 = 6, 14 − 6 = 8; 5 + 10 = 15, 10 + 5 = 15, 15 − 5 = 10, 15 − 10 = 5

Page 35

1. 12 − 3 = 9   2. 14 − 3 = 11
3. 15 − 3 = 12   4. 18 − 10 = 8
5. 5 + 4 + 6 = 15
6. 4 + 2 + 5 = 11

Page 36

1. 89   2. 67   3. 66   4. 49
5. 39   6. 48   7. 29   8. 47
9. 56   10. 58   11. 95   12. 76
13. 37

Page 37

Page 38

Page 39

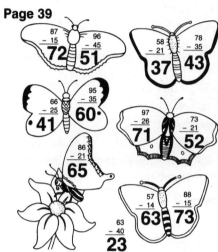

Page 43

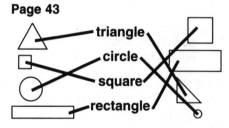

Drawings will vary.

Page 44

A. 3 triangles, 3 squares, 0 circles, 5 rectangles

B. 2 triangles, 2 squares, 6 circles, 4 rectangles

C. 2 triangles, 1 square, 4 circles, 5 rectangles

D. 4 triangles, 0 squares, 2 circles, 3 rectangles

Page 45

1. 4 cm   2. 3 cm   3. 6 cm
4. 12 cm   5. 5 cm   6. 7 cm
7. 4 cm

Page 46

1. 6 inches   2. 4 inches
3. 1 inch   4. 3 inches
5. 2 inches   6. 5 inches

Page 47

More than 1 liter—bathtub, soda bottle, pool

Less than 1 liter—pan, dropper, spoon, bottle, water pail

8 cups and 4 cups should be colored.

Page 48

A. 1, 6, 2

B. pencil, ribbon, needle and thread

C. 4, 8, 2

D. potatoes, oranges

Page 49

A. 2, 4, 3   B. 4, 3, 2

C.

Page 50

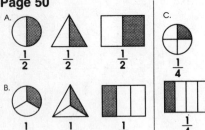

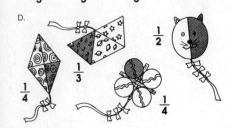

Page 53

1. 15 – 5 = 10, 10
2. 15 – 9 = 6, 6
3. 15 – 6 = 9, 9
4. 15 – 8 = 7, 7
5. 15 – 7 = 8, 8
6. 15 – 10 = 5, 5
7. 20 – 15 = 5

Page 54

A. penny   B. penny

C. dime   D. nickel

E. nickel   F. dime

G. dime   H. nickel

Page 55

A. 51¢, 46¢   B. 57¢, 28¢

C. 66¢, 80¢   D. 85¢, 62¢

Page 56

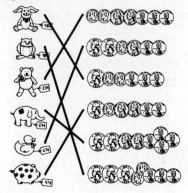

Page 57

A. 60¢   B. 66¢   C. 81¢

D. 69¢   E. 53¢

Page 58

A. 32¢, no   B. 51¢, yes

C. 62¢, no   D. 47¢, no

E. 44¢, yes   F. 48¢, no

G. 80¢, yes

Page 59

A. 2 dimes, 2 nickels

B. 1 dime, 5 nickels

C. 1 quarter, 1 penny

D. 3 nickels

E. 1 quarter, 2 nickels

F. 1 quarter, 4 pennies

Page 60

A. 15¢   B. 7¢   C. 3¢

D. 9¢   E. 12¢   F. 15¢

Page 65

1. Sunday   2. Monday
3. Tuesday   4. Wednesday
5. Thursday   6. Friday
7. Saturday

Page 66

1. Tuesday—3rd
2. Sunday—1st
3. Thursday—5th
4. Monday—2nd
5. Wednesday—4th
6. Saturday—7th
7. Friday—6th
8. Saturday
9. Tuesday
10. Thursday
11. Answers will vary.

Page 67

1. May   2. 31
3. Monday   4. 7

5. Monday   6. 18
7. 5   8. 5, 12, 19, 26
9. Thursday

Page 68

1. January   2. February
3. March   4. April
5. May   6. June
7. July   8. August
9. September   10. October
11. November   12. December

Page 69

1. 3:00   2. 8:00   3. 10:00
4. 6:00   5. 2:30   6. 4:30
7. 6:30   8. 9:30   9. 12:30

Page 70

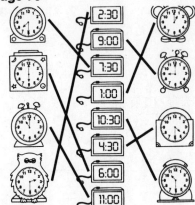

Page 71

A. eight-thirty, 8:30
B. three-thirty, 3:30
C. eleven o'clock, 11:00
D. four o'clock, 4:00
E. nine o'clock, 9:00
F. twelve-thirty, 12:30
G. six-thirty, 6:30
H. twelve o'clock, 12:00

Page 72

Answers will vary.

Page 73

1. 2:00, 3:00, 4:00
2. 6:00, 7:00, 8:00
3. 11:30, 12:30, 1:30
4. 3:30, 4:30, 5:30

Page 74

1. 4:00, 4:30   2. 8:30, 9:00
3. 6:30, 7:00   4. 10:30, 11:00
5. 3:00, 3:30   6. 1:30, 2:00

Page 75

1. 2 hours   2. 1 hour
3. 8:30   4. 7:30